Iron Horses

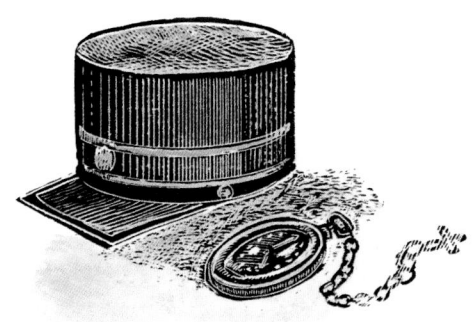

For Kristyn, Charles, Mikayla and Rayana—
*my four wonderful grandchildren—*V. K.

*To my brother Christopher Matson—*M. McC.

The art was done in scratchboard and watercolor.

Text copyright © 1999 by Verla Kay. Illustrations copyright © 1999 by Michael McCurdy

Published simultaneously in Canada. Printed in Hong Kong by South China Printing Co. (1988) Ltd.
Designed by Gunta Alexander. Text set in New Aster.
Library of Congress Cataloging-in-Publication Data
Kay, Verla. Iron Horses / by Verla Kay; illustrated by Michael McCurdy. p. cm.
Summary: Illustrations and simple rhyming text depict the race to construct railroads across the country
during the second half of the nineteenth century. [1. Railroads—Fiction. 2. Stories in rhyme.]
I. McCurdy, Michael, ill. II. Title. PZ8.3.K225Ir 1999 [E]—dc21 98-29898 CIP AC ISBN 0-399-23119-6
1 3 5 7 9 10 8 6 4 2
First Impression

IRON HORSES

BY **VERLA KAY** ✦ ILLUSTRATED BY **MICHAEL McCURDY**

G. P. PUTNAM'S SONS ✦ NEW YORK

Piercing whistles,
Shrieking wheels.
Hot steam hissing,
High-pitched squeals.

Huffing, puffing,
Smoking stacks.
Screeching, stopping,
End of tracks.

Railroad barons,
Visions, dreams.
Thinking, planning,
Plotting schemes.

Politicians,
Congress, vote.
"Build your railroad,"
Lincoln wrote.

Survey parties,
Canvas tents.
Levels, transits—
Measurements.

Work train, flatcars,
Blacksmith shop.
Kitchen, bunkhouse—
Sleep on top.

Thumping, bumping,
Ties and rails.
Clanging, banging,
Spikes and nails.

Rugged mountains,
Giant rifts.
Ragged, jagged,
Rocky cliffs.

Burly Irish,
Setting tracks.
Building trestles,
Bridging gaps.

Massive outcrop,
Blocking way.
Chinese, long ropes,
Baskets sway.

Blasting powder,
Rocks in air.
Shattered shale—
Everywhere.

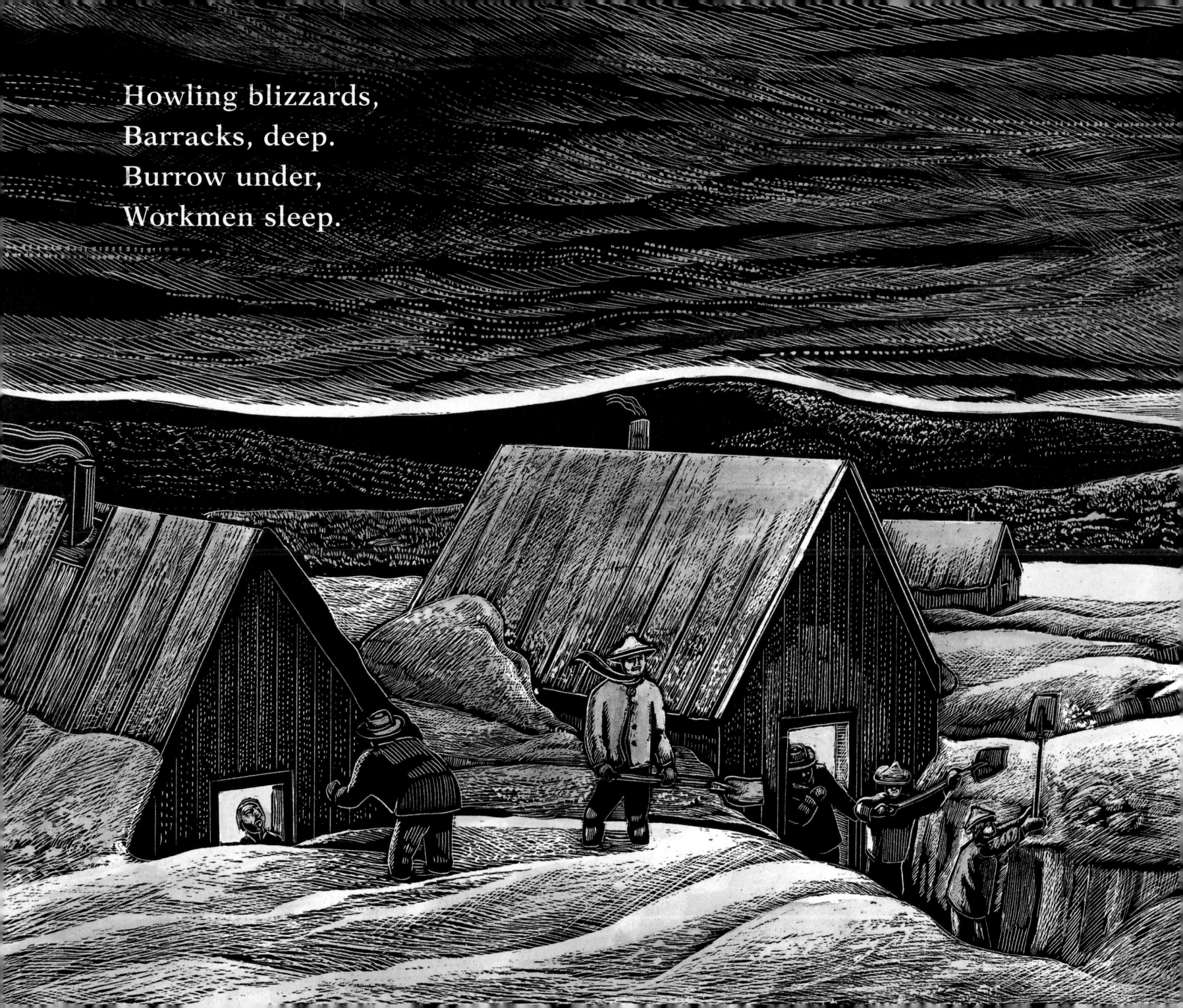

Howling blizzards,
Barracks, deep.
Burrow under,
Workmen sleep.

Piling snowdrifts,
Freezing rain.
Shoving, pushing,
Snowplow train.

Granite mountain,
Tunnel through.
High Sierras,
Flowers, blue.

Black clouds scuttle,
Billow high.
Lightning crackles,
Splitting sky.

Time for pleasure,
Town of tents.
Raucous ruckus,
Ladies. Gents.

East gang, West gang,
Racing fast.
Stubborn railroads,
Went right past!

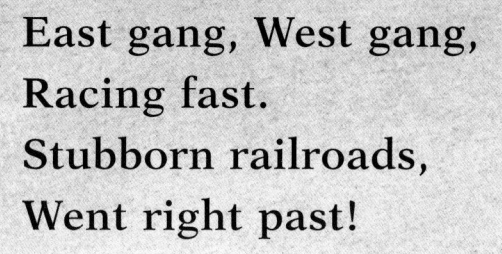

Joined in Utah,
End of race.
Ceremony,
Spikes in place.

Iron horses,
Burning oak.
Belching cinders,
Spewing smoke.

No more clippers,
Seasick folks,
Covered wagons,
Broken yokes.

Train tracks finished,
East to West.
People smiling,
"This is best."

CENTRAL PACIFIC RAILROAD

Promontory, Utah

UNION PACIFIC RAILROAD

Sacramento, California

Omaha, Nebraska

SIERRA NEVADA
MOUNTAINS

ROCKY
MOUNTAINS

AUTHOR'S NOTE ✦ When Congress passed the Pacific Railroad Act in 1862, two companies took on the responsibility of completing the first transcontinental rail line. The Central Pacific Railroad started pounding eastward from Sacramento, California on January 8, 1863. On November 5, 1865 the Union Pacific Railroad began charging west from Omaha, Nebraska and the race was on. Sometimes they moved forward only a few inches a day and at other times they progressed at an astonishing rate. On April 28, 1869 the Central Pacific spiked over ten miles of track in just twelve hours! That same year the railroads were so intense about the race that they blasted 200 miles past each other, each wanting to add as many miles of track to their total as they could. But Congress put a stop to this and on May 10, 1869 the tracks were joined at Promontory Summit, Utah. Now the trip from Missouri to California, which had taken up to six months by wagon train, could be completed in just six days.